beagle

understanding and
caring for your breed

Written by
Diana Porter

beagle

understanding and
caring for your breed

Written by
Diana Porter

Magnet & Steel Limited

Unit 6 Vale Business Park, Llandow, Vale of Glamorgan CF71 7PF.

Printed and bound in China through Printworks Global Limited.

All rights reserved. No part of this work may be reproduced, in any form or by any means, electronic or mechanical, including photocopying, recording or by any information storage and retrieval system, without the prior written permission of the publisher.

Copyright © Magnet & Steel Limited 2019

Every reasonable care has been taken in the compilation of this publication. The Publisher and Author cannot accept liability for any loss, damage, injury or death resulting from the keeping of Beagles by user(s) of this publication, or from the use of any materials, equipment, methods or information recommended in this publication or from any errors or omissions that may be found in the text of this publication or that may occur at a future date, except as expressly provided by law.

The 'he' pronoun is used throughout this book instead of the rather impersonal 'it', however no gender bias is intended.

ISBN: 978-1-910488-33-1

Contents

Introducing the Beagle

Smart, jaunty and bright as a button, the Beagle is the perfect family companion. Bred as a pack hound to track hare, he has a formidable sense of smell and where his nose leads, he will follow...

Physical characteristics

The Beagle is a medium-sized hound with a sturdy, compact body, built entirely without exaggeration. When hunting hare, he needed to keep going at a gallop for miles on end so he is an active, athletic dog with loads of stamina.

His head is powerful without being coarse with a domed skull and a square-cut muzzle. The ears are long, providing a perfect frame for his face. As you would expect in a scenthound, the nose is large with well-developed nostrils but the eyes are the

outstanding feature. They are large, and may be dark brown or hazel depending on coat colour. The amiable, heartwarming expression that comes from the eyes sums up the Beagle temperament.

Another Beagle feature is the tail or stern; this is high-set and carried gaily so dogs could be seen when tracking in long grass. Easy-going movement is essential for a scenthound needing to cover long distances with his nose to the ground. Typically, a Beagle moves with long-reaching strides, with the drive coming from the hindquarters.

If you have a predeliction for choosing the colour of your dog, the Beagle is the breed for you! There are 22 colour combinations to choose from, encompassing all the hound colours, which include tricolour (black, tan and white), blue, white and tan, badger pied, hare pied, lemon pied, lemon and white, tan and white, black and white and all white.

Temperament

The Beagle is a dream dog to live with: easy-going, sociable and affectionate. The Breed Standard, which is a description of the perfect Beagle, uses a number of adjectives to describe his characteristics and these are worth looking at in more detail:

Merry: This is a lovely term and it fully sums up the

Beagle's happy-go-lucky approach to life.

Bold: The Beagle was bred to work on his own initiative and he carries this through to domestic life; he is never afraid to make decisions – even when they may not comply with your wishes...

Alert: Life is full of interest for the inquisitive Beagle and he will be more than ready to investigate every new sight, sound and scent he comes across.

Intelligent: The Beagle is a clever dog and is adept at learning new skills. He is also something of a problem solver which he may well use to his own ends – particularly if it involves getting hold of illicit food...

Even temperament: This may sound bland but it is an outstanding quality in a companion dog. Every day is a good day for a Beagle, and he generally finds life pleasing and problem-free.

Amiable: The Beagle is a mild-mannered, sweet-tempered dog, and this makes him an absolute pleasure to live with.

The ideal home

The Beagle is an adaptable breed and will thrive in most households. He is a loving and affectionate dog, and will enjoy being included in family activities. He will be happy living in the town or in the country, in a mansion or in an apartment, as long as he is given sufficient exercise.

It is important to remember that the Beagle is governed by his sense of smell – and this can lead him astray. Your Beagle needs the opportunity to exercise, but he needs safe, enclosed areas if he is to be let off the lead. He is a determined character and no matter how good your recall is at home, he cannot be trusted in the great outdoors. There may be exceptions to the rule but it is always better to be safe than sorry.

As a pack-hound, the Beagle is highly sociable and will be delighted if you add to your canine population – particularly if it is a like-minded Beagle. However, if you prefer to have a lone dog, a Beagle will not object to being the centre of attention. One of the legacies of being a pack-hound is the Beagle's vocal range. Pack dogs frequently 'give tongue' when they are in pursuit of quarry, and the Beagle does like the sound of his own voice. Bear in mind that you have a clever dog on your hands, so providing mental stimulation is essential. If you can combine this with a comfortable bed, plentiful food and the opportunity to use his nose, your Beagle will be in heaven!

Facing page: The Beagle believes in enjoying life to the full!

Tracing back in time

The Beagle has a long and distinguished history as a hunting dog, prized for his stamina, his determination, and his amazing ability to follow a scent.

The origins of the Beagle are obscure but is is thought that the first hounds used for hunting small game were found in southern Europe, most particularly in Greece. There is written evidence from the Greek author, Xenophon, who was born around 433 BC. He lived in Corinth and when he retired from military duties he kept a pack of hounds – and he knew every hound by name.

The quarry was hare or rabbit and beaters would go forward followed by the hounds who drove the game towards nets. When in pursuit of small game, the huntsmen were on foot rather than on horseback.

Reaching Britain

The Romans were quick to find a use for the packs of hunting dogs they found in Europe; they were an easy means of providing hares and rabbits for their legions of soldiers. When they expanded their empire to Britain, they took packs of small hounds with them. In time, they were joined by larger hounds from Normandy and for the next few centuries hunting larger game, such as deer and boar, on horseback proved more popular.

However the smaller hounds survived and in the 14th century there is reference to "small houndes" belonging to the Prioress in Chaucer's Canterbury Tales. In Tudor times, Elizabeth I had a pack of "singing Beagles", named for their vocalisation when hunting; the dogs were said to be small enough to fit inside a lady's gauntlet.

Establishing a type

By the turn of the 19th century, there was a variety of Beagle type hounds that were used for hunting. There were Southern Beagles, Northern Beagles, and Cotswold Beagles; some were wire-haired and some were smooth-haired. There was also much inter-breeding between Harriers and other hounds; the Kerry Hound from Ireland may have been added to the mix. This black and tan dog, resembling a miniature Bloodhound, is thought to have contributed to the Beagle's scenting ability.

American links

Beagles first arrived in the USA around 1640. At this this time, they looked very different from the Beagle we know today. There are reports of hounds that looked more like Dachshunds, although they had straight legs.

The Beagle was particularly popular in the southern states but the Civil War (1861-1865) put a stop to all hunting activities. When the war ended, breeders once again turned to England to import new stock which would revive the breed.

A variety of hounds were used to develop the Beagle.

Developing
the breed

By the middle of the 19th century the Beagle was losing his distinctive appearance, and he was in danger of becoming nothing more than a miniature Foxhound. It was important that the Beagle's hunting abilities were preserved but steps had to be taken to allow the breed to survive in its own right.

Matters were brought to a head when the first Beagles were exhibited in the show ring in 1884. It was clear that there was no uniformity of type and this led to breed enthusiasts forming the Beagle Club of England in 1890.

At this time, hunting was controlled by the Association of Masters of Harriers and Beagles, but its judges could not agree on the salient breed points. So the Beagle Club of England's first task was to draw up a scale of points. This was accepted by the Kennel Club and, with very few changes, it remains the blueprint for the breed today.

The first Beagle to become a Champion was a bitch called Belton Scornful who gained her title in 1926.

As the breed developed, the very best dogs from hunting packs were used for breeding and these were combined with Beagles who were successful in the show ring.

This gave the breed a solid foundation, promoting dogs without exaggeration who were sound in mind and body.

Across the Atlantic, it was a similar story. In 1885 Blunder became the first Beagle to be registered in the American Kennel Club's stud book, and in 1888 the National Beagle Club was founded.

A Breed Standard was drawn up and the breed went from strength to strength. At the 1917 Westminster Show, there was an entry of 75 Beagles!

Interestingly, American breed enthusiasts agreed that there should be two sizes of Beagle, and to this day the two varieties are shown in separate classes.

The modern Beagle

As the 20th century progressed, hunting activities started to decline and packs of hounds were disbanded. Today the sport is kept alive in the form of drag hunting which is popular in the UK and Australia. In the USA, Field Trials are organised for Beagles and the title of Field Trial Champion is held in high regard.

Today, there is something of a divide between the working Beagle and those that are bred for the show ring. Working dogs need to be able to track over their local terrain so a larger, rangier dog will be better suited to hunt over the high stiles and stone walls encountered on moorland whereas a smaller, faster Beagle will excel on less challenging land.

The show Beagle, which encompasses the pet Beagle as most come from show lines, is likely to be heavier in build, with longer, low-set ears and a more square-cut muzzle.

However, it is important that the Beagle remains fit for function as this ensures that he is built on athletic lines and remains true to his original purpose.

Although, the Beagle's hunting ability is largely redundant, his outstanding sense of smell has found another use in current times.

In Australia, New Zealand and the USA Beagles are used to check passengers and their luggage at airports to detect if illegal food substances have been imported. Dogs are trained to run over suitcases as they are unloaded from the plane and to sit beside any suspicious case or person to alert their handlers.

Today the Beagle is well established throughout the world, valued by some for his hunting ability, by others for his role as a sniffer dog, and he also has a big following in the show world.

However, few would dispute that the Beagle's most important role is as a companion dog – and in this he is second to none.

The Beagle is now established as a worldwide favourite.

What should a Beagle look like?

The Beagle is a down-sized version of the Foxhound, a larger rangier dog and, as the name suggests, used primarily to hunt fox. However, the Beagle is very much a breed in his own right with the conformation that would allow him to hunt hare and rabbit. His compact, muscular body conveys athleticism and stamina – this is a dog that could hunt his quarry all day long.

The companion Beagle leads a very different life from his working forebears, but he should have the physical capabilities – and the temperament – to carry out his original role.

To achieve this, breeders are guided by a Breed

Standard, which is a written blueprint describing the perfect specimen.

Of course, there is no such thing as a 'perfect' dog, but breeders aspire to produce dogs that conform as closely as possible to the picture in words presented by the Breed Standard.

In the show ring, judges use the Breed Standard to assess the dogs that come before them, and it is the dog that, in their opinion, comes closest to the ideal, that will win top honours.

This has significance beyond the sport of showing, for it is the dogs that win in the ring which will be used for breeding.

The winners of today are therefore responsible for passing on their genes to future generations and preserving the breed in its best form.

There are some differences in the wording of the Breed Standard depending on national kennel clubs; the American Kennel Club and the Federation Cynologique Internationale, which is the governing body for 86 countries, have far more descriptive Standards than the brief outline given in the English version. The American Standard also differs as it allows for two varieties of Beagle depending on size.

General appearance

The Beagle should appear solid in build; he is sturdy and compact giving an impression of quality without coarseness. He is described as a "merry hound" and this is a perfect description of this most appealing of breeds.

Temperament

Bold, alert and determined, the Beagle has the true focus of a hunting dog, but he is also out-going and amiable without a trace of aggression or timidity.

Head

For a dog of his size, the Beagle has a distinctive head which is powerful without being coarse. It should be easy to tell male from female; the female is noticeably finer in feature. The skull is slightly domed and is moderately wide. The stop, the step-up between the muzzle and the forehead, is well-defined. The muzzle is of medium length and is square-cut. The nose is broad, preferably black, although less pigment is permissible in lighter-coloured hounds.

Eyes

The Beagle has the most appealing expression which comes from his large eyes which are set well apart.

A "merry hound" that gives an impression of quality.

They should be neither deep-set nor prominent. The colour may be dark brown or hazel depending on coat colour.

Ears

The long ears, with rounded tips, frame the face and give the Beagle his very distinctive look.

The ears should be set moderately low and when drawn out should reach to the nose, or close to it. They are fine in texture and hang gracefully close to the cheeks.

Mouth

The jaws are strong and teeth meet with a perfect scissor bite – the teeth on the upper jaw closely overlapping with the teeth on the lower jaw. The teeth are strong and white and the lips are close-fitting.

Neck

The Beagle is a scent hound; he therefore needs a strong, muscular neck of sufficient length to allow his nose to come down easily and effortlessly on a scent and to maintain this position while on the move.

The throat is clean and free from folds of skin.

Forequarters

The shoulders are sloping and well laid back. They are muscular but should not be heavy or loaded which would restrict freedom of movement.

The chest is deep and broad; the forelegs are straight and upright with elbows that turn neither in nor out. The height to the elbow is equivalent to about half the height at the wither (the highest point of the shoulder).

Body

The topline is straight and level, and although the back is relatively short it is strong and muscular with powerful loins. The chest reaches down below the elbows and the ribcage is well sprung which allows for plenty of lung room, essential for a dog built for endurance.

Hindquarters

The Beagle has muscular thighs and the stifles (knees) are well bent. The hocks (ankles) are parallel to each other and are moderately bent.

Tail

The Beagle's tail or 'stern' is a feature of the breed. It is sturdy and moderately long, set on high, and carried gaily with a slight curve. It should not be curled over the back or incline forwards at the root, and it should be well covered with hair, particularly on the underside.

Coat

The perfect hound coat is short, dense and waterproof. It should be smooth and hard to the touch, but not wiry.

Colour

The American Breed Standard states that all hound colours are acceptable but the English Standard is more specific, detailing all the colours, and stating that all, with the exception of all-white, may be mottled.

Regardless of colour or markings, Beagles have a white tip to their tails.

Movement

The Beagle has an even, lengthy stride. Keeping his back level, he drives from behind with long-reaching strides in front.

Size

In the UK, the desirable minimum height for a Beagle is 33cm (13in) at the wither, with a maximum height of 40cm (16in). In the USA, two varieties are allowed: 13in – for Beagles not exceeding 13in (33cm) and 15in – for Beagles over 13in but not exceeding 15in (38cm).

Summing up

Although the majority of Beagles are kept as pet dogs and will never be exhibited in the show ring, it is important that breeders strive for perfection and try to produce dogs that adhere as closely as possible to the Breed Standard.

This is the best way of ensuring that the Beagle remains sound in mind and body, and retains the characteristics that are unique to this very special breed.

The Beagle has a short, dense coat and comes in a variety of colours.

What do you want from your Beagle?

There are over 200 dog breeds to choose from, so how can you be sure that the Beagle is the right breed for you? Before you decide on a Beagle you need to be 100 per cent confident that this is the breed that is best suited to your lifestyle.

Companion

Gentle and affectionate, the Beagle is an outstanding companion dog – but don't be fooled into thinking that life with a Beagle is a breeze. This is a breed who is clever, inquisitive and determined – so you will need to keep one step ahead of this lovable rogue!

If you have a family with small children, the Beagle will be in his element, as long as you supervise interactions, ensuring he is not too boisterous.

He will prove to be an excellent playmate for children of all ages, but mutual respect must be established so that he is neither taunted nor teased, and he learns to co-operate with all members of his family.

This is a breed for active owners, so if you are getting on in years, or cannot easily provide exercise opportunities, he may not be an ideal choice.

Sports dog

If you want to get involved in one of the canine sports, you need to be realistic in your expectations. The Beagle certainly has the intelligence to learn, but he needs the motivation.

If you can get your Beagle turned on to a favourite toy or, more likely, extra tasty treats, he will become a willing partner.

Beagles have made their mark in many of the canine disciplines including obedience, agility and heelwork to music.

For more information, see Opportunities for Beagles.

Show dog

Do you have ambitions to exhibit your Beagle in the show ring? This is a highly competitive sport, with big entries in all the classes, so you do need the right dog to begin with.

If you plan to show your Beagle you need to track down a show quality puppy, and train him so he will perform in the show ring, and accept the detailed 'hands on' examination which is an essential part of the judging process.

It is also important to bear in mind that not every puppy with show potential develops into a top-quality specimen, and so you must be prepared to love your Beagle and give him a home for life, even if he doesn't make the grade.

It may take a little longer to find a show quality puppy.

What does your Beagle want from you?

A dog cannot speak for himself, so we need to view the world from a canine perspective and work out what a Beagle needs in order to live a happy, contented and fulfilling life.

Time and commitment

First of all, a Beagle needs a commitment that you will care for him for the duration of his life, guiding him through his puppyhood, enjoying his adulthood, and being there for him in his later years. If all potential owners were prepared to make this pledge, there would be scarcely any dogs in rescue.

The Beagle is a terrific companion dog, but this comes at a price. He loves to be with his own special

people, and this means that he will be thoroughly miserable if he is excluded from family activities, or expected to spend lengthy periods on his own. You will be left in no doubt as to his displeasure; a Beagle that is left on his own can be extremely destructive, he may be dirty or he may exercise his vocal cords and drive neighbours to distraction with continual howling.

It is important that all dogs can cope with spending some time on their own so they don't become anxious in this situation, but the maximum time a dog should be left is four hours.If this does not fit in with your lifestyle, you should delay owning a dog until your circumstances change.

Practical matters

The Beagle is a low maintenance dog when it comes to looking after him. His short coat needs minimal grooming and he is easy to please at mealtimes. However, he does need a reasonable amount of exercise. He can be adaptable in the sense that he does not have to follow his forebears and run for miles and miles.

But he does need the physical exercise to keep him in trim, and, almost as importantly, he needs the mental stimulation which comes from exploring new places and investigating those enticing scents...

Leadership

The Beagle does not seek to assert his authority; he is an easy-going dog who enjoys being in the hub of family activities. However, he is very far from being stupid and he will use his intelligence to please himself unless he is given appropriate guidance.

It is your job to show your Beagle how you want him to behave by rewarding the behaviour that you consider desirable. You need to be 100 per cent consistent, so your Beagle is left in no doubt as to what is deemed acceptable.

If he pushes the boundaries or misbehaves – refusing to budge from the sofa, for example - interrupt his undesirable behaviour by ignoring him or refocusing his attention with a toy or a treat.

As soon as your Beagle makes the 'right' decision and changes his behaviour, you can reward him handsomely. In this way, your Beagle learns good manners without the need for force or coercion. He is living with you in peace and harmony because he loves and respects you.

Extra
considerations

Now you have decided that a Beagle is the dog of your dreams, you can narrow your choice so you know exactly what you are looking for.

Male or female?

The choice of male or female Beagle comes down to personal preference. Although the sexes are easy to tell apart, there is not necessarily a difference in size. Generally speaking, females are quicker to mature and may be more independent-minded than males. Owners report that males are the soft and soppy ones and will enjoy no end of petting.

If you opt for a female, you will need to cope with her seasons, which will start at any time from six months onwards and will occur approximately every six months thereafter.

During the three-week period of a season, you will need to keep your bitch away from entire males (males that have not been neutered) to eliminate the risk of an unwanted pregnancy. Some owners also report that females may be a little moody and withdrawn during their seasonal cycle.

Many pet owners opt for neutering, which puts an end to the seasons, and also and has many attendant health benefits. The operation, known as spaying, is usually carried out at some point after the first season. The best plan is to seek advice from your vet.

An entire male may not cause many problems, although some do have a stronger tendency to mark, which could include inside the house. However, training will usually put a stop to this. An entire male will also be on the lookout for bitches in season, and this may lead to difficulties, depending on your circumstances.

Neutering (castrating) a male is a relatively simple operation, and there are associated health benefits. Again, you should seek advice from your vet.

Colour?

Health and temperament should be top of your list of priorities, but you may well have a preference for a particular colour. The Beagle comes in a wide range of colours and markings, but the most common are tricolour (black, tan and white), tan and white followed by lemon and white.

A blanketed tricolour is often requested, and this certainly looks very smart, particularly if you are planning to exhibit your Beagle in the show ring. This takes the form of a tan hound with a white muzzle, blaze, throat, chest, legs and tip of the tail, and a black blanket or saddle across the back.

The black area may be solid or it can be broken, known as an open-marked tri. It is worth pointing out that tris are born black and white; the tan colouring comes through gradually. In fact black and white Beagles are very rare. Tan and white Beagles and lemons are born almost white; the markings develop as the coat changes.

Mottled Beagles can be any colour; the pattern is heavily spotted and can give a blue appearance.

More than one?

The Beagle is a pack hound and he loves the company of his own kind. That said, he is a sociable dog and will get along with any breed, but there is nothing like having a companion that shares your mind-set!

The Beagle can become over-dependent on his 'people' and develop separation anxiety if he is left on his own. A second dog can solve this problem, but you cannot rely on it. If a Beagle has become needy, he may still be anxious when his humans are absent – even if he has a canine companion.

Unlike many other breeds, same sex Beagle combinations get on just as well as a male/female pair.

It may be that two females egg each other on to become more independent whereas two males are more likely to be home-loving softies – but all Beagles are individuals so it is a matter of biding your time and seeing what you have on your hands.

Obviously if you opt for a male and a female, one or both dogs will need to be neutered. When it comes to choosing a puppy, be wary of a breeder who encourages you to buy two pups from the same litter, as it is unlikely that the welfare of the puppies is their top priority.

You may think that rearing two puppies at the same time will be half the trouble – but you could not be more wrong. The puppies will bond with each other rather than with you, and training will be a nightmare unless you separate the dogs and teach them individually.

Facing page: Lemon and white Beagles are growing in popularity.

Most responsible breeders have a waiting list of potential purchasers before a litter is even born and have no need to make this type of sale.

If you do decide to take on a second Beagle, wait at least 18 months so your first dog is fully trained and settled before embarking on a puppy.

An older dog

You may decide to miss out on the puppy phase and take on an older dog instead. Such a dog may be harder to track down, but sometimes a breeder may have a youngster that is not suitable for showing, but is perfect for a family pet.

In some cases, a breeder may rehome a female when her breeding career is at an end so she will enjoy the benefits of more individual attention.

There are advantages to taking on an older dog, as you know exactly what you are getting. But the upheaval of changing homes can be quite upsetting, so you will need to have plenty of patience during the settling in period.

Rehoming a rescued dog

We are fortunate that the number of Beagles that end up in rescue is relatively small. However, there are always some Beagles that need rehoming through no fault of their own. The reasons are various, ranging from illness or death of the original owner to family breakdown, changing jobs, or even the arrival of a new baby.

You are unlikely to find a Beagle in an all-breed rescue centre; contacting a specialist breed club that runs a rescue scheme will be your best option if you decide to go down this route.

Try to find out as much as you can about a dog's history so you know exactly what you are taking on. You need to be aware of age and health status, likes and dislikes, plus any behavioural issues that may be relevant.

You need to be realistic about what you are capable of achieving so you can be sure you can give the dog in question a permanent home.

Regardless of the dog's previous history, you will need to give him plenty of time and be patient with him as he settles into his new home.

It may take weeks, or even months before he becomes fully integrated in the family, but if all goes well you will have the reward of knowing that you have given a Beagle a second chance.

Sourcing
a puppy

Your aim is to find a healthy puppy that is typical of the breed, and has been reared with the greatest possible care. Where do you start?

A tried and trusted method of finding a puppy is to attend a dog show where your chosen breed is being exhibited.

This will give you the opportunity to see lots of different Beagles. You will see the different colours, and when you look closely you will detect that there are different 'types' on show. They are all pure-bred Beagles, but breeders produce dogs with a family likeness, so you can see which type you prefer.

When judging has been completed, talk to the exhibitors and find out more about their dogs. They may not have puppies available, but some will be planning a litter, and you may decide to put your name on a waiting list.

Internet research

The Internet is an excellent resource, but when it comes to finding a puppy, use it with care:

DO go to the website of your national kennel club.

Both the American Kennel Club (AKC) and the Kennel Club (KC) have excellent websites which will give you information about the Beagle as a breed, and what to look for when choosing a puppy.

You will also find contact details for specialist breed clubs (see opposite).

Both sites have lists of puppies available, and you can look out for breeders of merit (AKC) and assured breeders (KC) which indicates that a code of conduct has been adhered to.

DO find details of specialist breed clubs.

On breed club websites you will find lots of useful information which will help you to care for your Beagle. There may be contact details of breeders in your area, or you may need to go through the club secretary.

Some websites also have a list of breeders that have puppies available. The advantage of going through a breed club is that members will follow a code of ethics, and this will give you some guarantees regarding breeding stock and health checks.

If you are planning to show your Beagle you will obviously go to a breeder that has had some success in the ring, so you will need to do additional research to discover more about their breeding lines and the type of Beagle they produce.

DO NOT look at puppies for sale.

There are legitimate Beagle breeders with their own websites and they may, occasionally, advertise a litter, although in most cases reputable breeders have waiting lists for their puppies. The danger comes from unscrupulous breeders that produce puppies purely for profit, with no thought for the health of the dogs they breed from and no care given to rearing the litter.

Photos of puppies are hard to resist, but never make a decision based purely on an advertisement. You need to find out who the breeder is, and have the opportunity to visit their premises and inspect the litter before making a decision.

Questions, questions, questions

When you find a breeder with puppies available, you will have lots of questions to ask. These should include the following:

- Where have the puppies been reared? Hopefully, they will be in a home environment which gives them the best possible start in life.

- How many are in the litter?

- What is the split of males and females?

- What colours are available?

- How many have already been spoken for? The breeder will probably be keeping a puppy to show or for breeding, and there may be others on a waiting list.

The breeder will be intent on finding the best possible puppy homes.

- Can I see the mother with her puppies?

- What age are the puppies?

- When will they be ready to go to their new homes?

Bear in mind puppies need to be with their mother and siblings until they are eight weeks of age otherwise they miss out on vital learning and communication skills, which will have a detrimental effect on them for the rest of their lives. You should also be prepared to answer a number of searching questions so the breeder can check if you are suitable as a potential owner of one of their precious puppies. You will be asked some or all of the following questions:

- What is your home set up?

- Do you have children/grandchildren?

- What are their ages?

- Do you have a securely-fenced garden?

- Is there somebody at home the majority of the time?

- What is your previous experience with dogs?

- Do you already have other dogs at home?

- Do you have plans to show your Beagle?

The breeder is not being intrusive; he needs to understand the type of home you will be able to provide in order to make the right match. Do not be offended by this; the breeder is doing it both for your, and the dog's, benefit.

Steer clear of a breeder who does not ask you questions. He or she may be more interested in making money out of the puppies than ensuring that they go to good homes.

They may also have taken other shortcuts, which may prove disastrous, and very expensive, in terms of vet bills or plain heartache.

Health issues

In common with all pure-bred dogs, the Beagle suffers from some hereditary problems so you need to talk to the breeder about the health status of breeding stock and find out if there are any issues of concern.

For information on inherited conditions, see Breed-specific disorders.

Puppy watching

Beagles puppies are totally irresistible. Looking like adults in miniature, they come running to greet you, tripping over their ears, and each puppy seems to be saying: "pick me!" However, you must not to let your heart rule your head.

Try to put your feelings to one side so that you can make an informed choice. You need to be 100 per cent confident that the breeding stock is healthy, and the puppies have been reared with love and care, before making a commitment to buy.

Viewing a litter

It is a good idea to have mental checklist of what to look out for when you visit a breeder. You want to see:

- A clean, hygienic environment.

- Puppies who are out-going, friendly, and eager to meet you.

- A sweet-natured mother who is ready to show off her pups.

- Puppies that are well covered, but not pot-bellied, which could be an indication of worms.

- Bright eyes, with no sign of soreness or discharge.

- Clean ears that smell fresh.

- No discharge from the ears or the nose.

- Clean rear ends – matting could indicate an upset tummy.

It is important that you see the mother with her puppies as this will give you a good idea of the temperament they are likely to inherit. It is also helpful if you can see other close relatives so you can see the type of Beagle the breeder produces.

In most cases, you will not be able to see the father (sire) as most breeders will travel some distance to find a stud dog that is not too close to their own bloodlines and complements their bitch.

However, you should be able to see photos of him and be given the chance to examine his pedigree and show record.

Companion puppy

If you are looking for a Beagle as a companion, you should be guided by the breeder who will have spent hours and hours puppy watching, and will know each of the pups as an individual. It is tempting to choose a puppy yourself, but the breeder will take into account your family set up and lifestyle and will help you to pick the most suitable puppy.

Show puppy

If you are buying a puppy with the hope of showing him, make sure you make this clear to the breeder. A lot of planning goes into producing a litter, and although all the puppies will have been reared with equal care, there will be one or two that have show potential.

Below: The breeder will know all the puppies as individuals.

Ideally, recruit a breed expert to inspect the puppies with you so you have the benefit of their objective evaluation.

The breeder will also be there to help as they will want to ensure that only the best of their stock is exhibited in the show ring.

Wait until the puppies are between seven and eight weeks before making your choice as this gives them time to develop.

By this stage, the tan colour should have come through on tricolours, and you will have a better idea of the markings on tan and whites and lemons.

In terms of conformation, the general shape and symmetry should be evident, although all puppies go through 'awkward' stages.

Even so, a puppy with show potential should appear compact and balanced with the correct tail-set which will allow the tail to be carried gaily.

The proportions of the head and the square-cut muzzle should be evident, along with the drop ears framing the face, and the melting expression coming from the eyes which is so typical of the Beagle.

Facing page: It takes an expert eye to evaluate show potential.

A Beagle-friendly home

It may seem an age before your Beagle puppy is ready to leave the breeder and move to his new home. But you can fill the time by getting your home ready, and buying the equipment you will need.

These preparations apply to a new puppy but, in reality, they are the means of creating an environment that is safe and secure for your Beagle throughout his life.

In the home

Nothing is safe when a puppy is about, and that is certainly true if you have a Beagle in the house! Everything is new and exciting for a young puppy,

and he will investigate with his mouth, which can lead him into all sorts of mischief.

One thing is certain; a free-ranging Beagle puppy cannot be trusted. Remember, it is not only your prized possessions that are under threat – the damage a puppy can inflict on himself is equally relevant.

Trailing electric cables are a major hazard so these will need to be secured out of reach. You will need to make sure all cupboards and storage units cannot be opened or broken into.

This applies particularly in the kitchen where you may store cleaning materials, and other substances which could be toxic to dogs.

There are a number of household plants that are poisonous, so these will need to relocated, along with breakable ornaments.

Bear in mind that the Beagle is an inveterate thief; he will think nothing of raiding bins and reaching up to table-tops and work services if he thinks tasty morsels are on offer.

The golden rule is to keep all food out of reach, and to keep the bin well-secured. It is especially important to keep your Beagle's food behind closed doors, particularly if you are feeding a complete diet. If your Beagle binges on dry food, it could have disastrous consequences.

You may decide to declare upstairs off-limits and this is a sensible decision, particularly as negotiating stairs can be hazardous for a young puppy.

The best way of doing this is to install a baby gate; these can also be useful if you want to restrict your Beagle's freedom in any other part of the house. This barrier works well as your dog is separate but does not feel excluded from what is going on.

In the garden

Beagles are great explorers and your puppy will not only investigate every nook and cranny of the garden, he will also try to find his way out to see what lies beyond!

Before your puppy arrives home make sure that your garden is securely fenced; a height of 1.5m (5 ft) is a minimum requirement. If you have gates leading out of your property, you will need to check that they have secure fastenings.

Remember, a Beagle is not confined to jumping out of the garden – he can always dig his way out... Beagles love to dig, which means that hedging is not a secure barrier.

You will have to enhance the boundary with additional fencing so that your dog cannot find a way through.

If you are a keen gardener, your Beagle will be happy to join you – but you may not be pleased with the results. Left to his own devises, he will dig up long-established shrubs with determination and enthusiasm, or get to work on the new plants you have just planted.

For this reason, it may be a good idea to fence off a section of the garden and keep it free from flowerbeds so your Beagle can be let out without constant supervision.

If you allow your Beagle free access to the garden, you need to bear in mind that there are a number of plants that are toxic to dogs which you will need to remove before your puppy comes home. These include tulip bulbs, lily of the valley, azaleas, jasmine and daffodil flowers; you can find a comprehensive list on the Internet.

You also need to be aware that garden chemicals, such as fertilisers, fungicides and pesticides, are highly toxic so be very careful where you use them.

Swimming pools and ponds should be covered, as most puppies are fearless and, although it is easy for a puppy to take the plunge, it is virtually impossible for him to get out, potentially with lethal consequences.

You will also need to designate a toileting area. This will assist the house training process, and it will also make cleaning up easier.

House rules

Before your puppy comes home, hold a family conference to make the house rules. You need to decide which rooms your puppy will have access to, and establish whether he is to be allowed on the furniture or not.

It is important to start as you mean to go on.

You cannot invite a puppy on to the sofa for cuddles only to decide in a few months' time that this is no longer desirable.

The Beagle likes to please, but he will push it if he doesn't know where his boundaries lie. If house rules are applied consistently, he will understand what is, and what is not, allowed, and he will learn to respect you and co-operate with you.

Buying equipment

There are some essential items of equipment you will need for your Beagle. If you choose wisely, much of it will last for many years to come.

Indoor crate

Rearing a puppy is so much easier if you invest in an indoor crate. It provides a safe haven for your puppy at night, when you have to go out during the day, and at other times when you cannot supervise him.

A puppy needs a base where he feels safe and secure, and where he can rest undisturbed. An indoor crate provides the perfect den, and many adults continue to use them throughout their lives. The ideal sized crate for a Beagle is 80cm x 54cm x 60cm (31.5in x 21in x 23.5in).

This gives a Beagle plenty of space to stand up and turn around and to sleep fully stretched out.

You will also need to consider where you are going to locate the crate. The kitchen is usually the most suitable place as this is the centre of family life.

Try to find a snug corner where the puppy can rest when he wants to, but where he can also see what is going on around him, and still be with the family.

Beds and bedding

The crate will need to be lined with bedding and the best type to buy is synthetic fleece. This is warm and cosy, and as moisture soaks through it, your puppy will not have a wet bed when he is tiny and still unable to go through the night without relieving himself. This type of bedding is machine washable and easy to dry; buy two pieces, so you have one to use while the other piece is in the wash.

If you have purchased a crate, you may not feel the need to buy an extra bed, although your Beagle may like to have a bed in the family room so he feels part of household activities.

There is an amazing array of dog-beds to chose from – duvets, bean bags, cushions, baskets, igloos, mini-four posters – so you can take your pick!

However, a Beagle puppy may also enjoy chewing his bed, so it may be worth delaying this purchase until he is beyond the teething phase. But be warned, some Beagles never outgrow the desire to chew, so you will be on a mission to find something indestructible...

Collar and lead

You may think that it is not worth buying a collar for the first few weeks, but the sooner your pup gets used to it, the better. A nylon lightweight collar is recommended as most puppies will accept it without making a fuss.

Be careful when you are fitting the collar that is not too tight, but equally not too loose as slipping the collar can become a favourite game...

It is worth investing in good-quality gear for your Beagle.

A thin, matching webbing lead will be fine to begin with; the last thing you want is for your puppy to feel weighed down by a heavy collar and lead. When your Beagle is fully grown, you can choose from the huge range of collars and leads that are available.

There are some stunning designs to choose from but your top priorities are comfort and security. The collar must be a good fit, the lead should be easy on the hand – and both should have secure fastenings.

An extending lead can be a useful purchase as you can give your Beagle limited freedom when it is not safe or permitted to allow him off lead.

However, you should never use it when walking alongside roads as an unexpected pull from your Beagle, resulting in the lead extending further than you want, could have disastrous consequences.

ID

Your Beagle needs to wear some form of ID when he is out in public places. This can be in the form of a disc, engraved with your contact details, attached to the collar.

When your Beagle is full-grown, you can buy an embroidered collar with your contact details, which eliminates the danger of the disc becoming detached from the collar.

Microchipping, which is a permanent form of ID, is now a legal requirement in the UK and increasingly breeders are getting puppies micro chipped before they go to their new homes.

A microchip is the size of a grain of rice. It is injected under the skin, usually between the shoulder blades, with a special needle. It has tiny barbs on it, which dig into the tissue around where it lies, so it does not migrate from that spot.

Each chip has its own unique identification number which can only be read by a special scanner.

That ID number is then registered on a national database with your name and details, so that if ever your dog is lost, he can be taken to any vet or rescue centre where he is scanned and then you are contacted.

If your puppy has not been micro chipped, you can ask your vet to do it, maybe when he goes for his vaccinations.

Bowls

Your Beagle will need two bowls; one for food, and one for fresh drinking water, which should always be readily available.

A stainless steel bowl is a good choice for food as it is tough and hygienic.

Plastic bowls will almost certainly be chewed, and there is an attendant danger of bacteria collecting in the small cracks that may appear. You can opt for a second stainless steel bowl for drinking water, or you may prefer a heavier ceramic bowl which will not be knocked over so easily.

Food

The breeder will let you know what your puppy is eating and should provide a full diet sheet to guide you through the first six months of your puppy's feeding regime – how much they are eating per meal, how many meals per day, when to increase the amounts given per meal and when to reduce the meals per day.

The breeder may provide you with some food when you go and collect your puppy, but it is worth making enquiries in advance about the availability of the brand that is recommended.

Grooming gear

The Beagle is a low maintenance breed in terms of coat but there are a few bare essentials you will need:

• Soft brush to use while your puppy is becoming accustomed to grooming.

Facing page: Ask the breeder for advice on diet.

- Bristle brush for the adult coat

- Hound glove/rubber brush for use at times of year when the coat is shedding

- Rake for removing dead hair

- Nail-clippers – the guillotine type are easy to use.

- Toothbrush and toothpaste: Choose between a long-handled toothbrush or a finger brush – whichever you find easiest to use. There are flavoured canine toothpastes on the market which are acceptable to your dog.

Toys

Beagle puppies love to play, and there is no shortage of dog toys on the market.

But before you get carried away with buying a vast range of toys to keep your puppy entertained, think about possible hazards. A puppy can easily chew bits from soft or plastic toys, and if this material is ingested it can cause serious problems in the form of a blockage.

The safest toys to choose are made of hard rubber; a rubber kong which can be stuffed with food is ideal. You can also buy rope tug toys, but be careful how you play with your dog, particularly while he is teething.

Finding a vet

Before your puppy arrives home, you should register with a vet. Visit several vets in your local area, or speak to other pet owners that you might know, to see who they recommend.

It is so important to find a good vet – almost as much as finding a good doctor for yourself. You need to find someone with whom you can build up a good rapport and have complete faith in. Word of mouth is really the best recommendation.

When you contact a veterinary practice, find out the following:

- Do they have an appointment system?

- What are the arrangements for emergency, out of hours cover?

- Do any of the vets in the practice have experience treating Beagles?

- What facilities are available at the practice?

If you are satisfied with what your find, and the staff appear to be helpful and friendly, book an appointment so your puppy can have a health check a couple of days after you collect him.

Settling in

When you first arrive home with your puppy, be careful not to overwhelm him. You and your family are hugely excited, but the puppy is in a completely strange environment with new sounds, smells and sights, which is a daunting experience, even for the boldest of pups.

Some puppies are very confident, wanting to play straightaway and quickly making friends; others need a little longer. Keep a close check on your puppy's body language and reactions so you can proceed at a pace he is comfortable with.

First, let him explore the garden. He will probably need to relieve himself after the journey home, so take him to the allocated toileting area and, when he performs, give him plenty of praise.

When you take your puppy indoors, let him investigate again. Show him his crate, and encourage him to go in by throwing in a treat.

Let him have a sniff, and allow him to go in and out as he wants to. Later on, when he is tired, you can put him in the crate while you stay in the room. In this way he will learn to settle and will not think he is being abandoned.

It is a good idea to feed your puppy in his crate, at least to begin with, as this helps to build up a positive association. It will not be long before your Beagle sees his crate as his own special den and will go there as a matter of choice. Some owners place a blanket over the crate, covering the back and sides, so that it is even more cosy and den-like.

Meeting the family

Resist the temptation of inviting friends and neighbours to come and meet the new arrival; your puppy needs to focus on getting to know his new family for the first few days. Try not to swamp your Beagle with too much attention; give him a chance to explore and find his feet. There will be plenty of time for cuddles later on!

If you have children in the family, you need to keep everything as calm as possible. Your puppy may not have met children before, and even if he has, he will still find them strange and unpredictable.

A puppy can become alarmed by too much noise, or

he may go to the opposite extreme and become over-excited, which can lead to mouthing and nipping.

The best plan is to get the children to sit on the floor and give them all a treat. Each child can then call the puppy, stroke him, and offer a treat.

In this way the puppy is making the decisions rather than being forced into interactions he may find stressful.

If he tries to nip or mouth, make sure there is a toy at the ready, so his attention can be diverted to something he is allowed to bite. If you do this consistently, he will learn to inhibit his desire to mouth when he is interacting with people.

Right from the start, impose a rule that the children are not allowed to pick up or carry the puppy. They can cuddle him when they are sitting on the floor. This may sound a little severe, but a wriggly puppy can be dropped in an instant, sometimes with disastrous consequences.

If possible, try to make sure your Beagle is only given attention when he has all four feet on the ground. This is a breed than can be attention seeking so if your pup learns that jumping up and demanding attention is not rewarding, it will pay dividends later on.

Involve all family members with the day-to-day

care of your puppy; this will enable the bond to develop with the whole family as opposed to just one person. Encourage the children to train and reward the puppy, teaching him to follow their commands without question.

The animal family

Great care must be taken when introducing a puppy to a resident dog to ensure that relations get off on the right footing. Beagles thrive on canine company so it is rare to have problems, but those early interactions are vital.

Your adult dog may be allowed to meet the puppy at the breeder's, which is ideal as the older dog will not feel threatened if he is away from home. But if this is not possible, allow your dog to smell the puppy's bedding (the bedding supplied by the breeder is fine) before they actually meet so he familiarises himself with the puppy's scent.

The garden is the best place for introducing the puppy, as the adult will regard it as neutral territory. He will probably take a great interest in the puppy and sniff him all over. Most puppies are naturally submissive in this situation, and your pup may lick the other dog's mouth or roll over on to his back. Try not to interfere as this is the natural way that dogs get to know each other.

You will only need to intervene if the older dog is too boisterous, and alarms the puppy. In this case, it is a good idea to put the adult on his lead so you have some measure of control.

It rarely takes long for an adult to accept a puppy, as he does not constitute a threat. This will be underlined if you make a big fuss of the older dog so that he has no reason to feel jealous. But no matter how well the two dogs are getting on, do not leave them alone unless one is crated.

Beagles enjoy the company of their own kind.

Feline friends

The Beagle is easy-going and tolerant and will learn to live peaceably with the family cat. There will always be the odd occasion when he can't resist a chase 'just for fun', but most of the time cat and dog will co-exist peacefully.

However, it is important to supervise early interactions so you establish the ground rules. It is much easier to instil good habits rather than trying to resolve a situation that has got out of hand. It may be easier if the cat is confined in a carrier for the first couple of meetings so your puppy has a chance to make his acquaintance in a controlled situation. Keep calling your puppy to you and rewarding him so that he does not focus too intently on the cat.

You can then graduate to holding your puppy while the cat is free, again rewarding him with a treat every time he responds to you and looks away from the cat. When you allow your puppy to go free, make sure the cat has an easy escape route, just in case he tries to chase. This is an on-going process but, all the time your Beagle is learning that he is rewarded for ignoring the cat. In time, the novelty will wear off and the pair will mostly ignore each other. In some cases, a Beagle and cat will become the best of friends and end up sharing a bed!

Facing page:
If you supervise
initial interactions,
your Beagle will learn
to live in peace with
the family cat.

Feeding

The breeder will generally provide enough food for the first few days so the puppy does not have to cope with a change in diet – and possible digestive upset – along with all the stress of moving home. Some puppies eat up their food from the first meal onwards, others are more concerned by their new surroundings and are too distracted to eat. The Beagle is a real foodie so it should not take him long to find his appetite.

The rule is to give him 10 minutes to eat what he wants and then remove the leftovers and start afresh at the next meal. Obviously if you have any concerns about your puppy in the first few days, seek advice from your vet. The Beagle is unlikely to become possessive over his food bowl but food is a big issue in his mind, and he needs to learn basic manners. First and foremost, his mealtimes should be respected by all members of the family.

He should be given the space to eat in peace; if you have children, you need to establish a rule that no one is to go near him when he is feeding. This is sound common sense, and removes all risk of problems arising, no matter how unintentional they may be.

At the same time, you need to teach your Beagle that

people do not pose a threat when he is eating. You can do this by giving him half his ration, and then dropping food around his bowl. This will stop him guarding his bowl and, at the same time, he will see your presence in a positive light. You can also call him away from the bowl and reward him with food – maybe something extra special – which he can take from your hand. Start doing this as soon as your puppy arrives in his new home, and continue working on it throughout his life.

The first night

Your puppy will have spent the first weeks of his life with either his mother or curled up with his siblings. He is then taken from everything he knows as familiar, lavished with attention by his new family, and then comes bed time when he is left all alone. It is little wonder that he feels abandoned.

The best plan is to establish a nighttime routine, and then stick to it so that your puppy knows what is expected of him. Take your puppy out into the garden to relieve himself, and then settle him in his crate. Some people leave a low light on for the puppy at night for the first week, others have tried a radio as company or a ticking clock. A covered hot-water bottle, filled with warm water, can also be a comfort. Like people, puppies are all individuals and what works for one, does not necessarily work for another, so it is a matter of trial and error. Be very positive when you leave your puppy on his own; do not linger, or keep returning; this will make the situation more difficult. It is inevitable that he will protest to begin with, but if you stick to your routine, he will accept that he gets left at night but you always return in the morning.

Rescued dogs

Settling an older, rescued dog in the home is very similar to a puppy in as much as you will need to make the same preparations regarding his homecoming. Like a puppy, an older dog will need you to be consistent, so start as you mean to go on.

There is often an initial honeymoon period when you bring a rescued dog home, where he will be on his best behaviour for the first few weeks. It is after these first couple of weeks that the true nature of the dog will show, so be prepared for subtle changes in his behaviour. It may be advisable to register with a reputable training club, so you can seek advice on any training or behavioural issues at an early stage.

Above all, remember that a rescued dog ceases to be a rescued dog the moment he enters his forever home and should be treated normally like any other family pet.

Facing page: A rescued Beagle will need patience and understanding as he settles into his new home.

House training

This is an aspect of training that first-time owners dread, but if you start as you mean to go on, it will not be long before your Beagle understands what is required.

The key to successful house training is vigilance and consistency. If you establish a routine, and you stick to it, your puppy will soon get the hang of it.

Equally, you must be there to supervise him at all times, except when he is safely tucked up in his crate. It is when a puppy is left to wander from room to room that accidents are most likely to happen.

As discussed earlier, you will have allocated a toileting area in your garden when preparing for your puppy's homecoming.

You need to take your puppy to this area every time

he needs to relieve himself so he builds up an association and knows why you have brought him out to the garden.

Establish a routine and make sure you take your puppy out at the following times:

- First thing in the morning

- After mealtimes

- On waking from a sleep

- Following a play session

- Last thing at night

A puppy should be taken out to relieve himself every two hours as an absolute minimum. If you can manage an hourly trip out, so much the better.

The more often your puppy gets it right, the quicker he will learn to be clean in the house. It helps if you use a verbal cue, such as 'Busy', when your pup is performing and, in time, this will trigger the desired response. Do not be tempted to put your puppy out on the doorstep in the hope that he will toilet on his own. Most pups simply sit there, waiting to get back inside the house!

No matter how bad the weather is, accompany your puppy and give him lots of praise when he performs correctly.

Do not rush back inside as soon as he has finished; your puppy might start to delay in the hope of prolonging his time outside with you. Praise him, have a quick game, and then you can both return indoors.

When accidents happen

No matter how vigilant you are, there are bound to be accidents. If you witness the accident, take your puppy outside immediately, and give him lots of praise if he finishes his business out there.

If you are not there when he has an accident, do not scold him when you discover what has happened. He will not remember what he has done and will not understand why you are cross with him. Simply clean it up and resolve to be more vigilant next time.

Make sure you use a deodoriser, available in pet stores, when you clean up otherwise your pup will be drawn to the smell and may be tempted to use the same spot again.

Choosing
a diet

There are so many different types of dog food on sale, all claiming to be the best, so how do you know what is likely to suit your Beagle?

When choosing a diet, there are basically three categories to choose from:

Complete

This is probably the most popular diet as it is easy to feed and is specially formulated with all the nutrients your dog needs. This means that you should not add any supplements or you may upset the nutritional balance.

Most complete diets come in different life stages: puppy, adult maintenance and senior, so this means that your Beagle is getting what he needs when he is growing, during adulthood, and as he becomes older.

You can even get prescription diets for dogs with particular health issues. Generally, an adult maintenance diet should contain 21 to 24 per cent protein and 10 to 14 per cent fat. Protein levels should be higher in puppy diets, and reduced in veteran diets.

There are many different brands to choose from so it is advisable to seek advice from your puppy's breeder who will have lengthy experience of feeding Beagles.

Canned/pouches

This type of food is usually fed with hard biscuit, and most Beagles find it very appetising. However, the ingredients and the nutritional value do vary significantly between the different brands so you will need to check the label.

This type of food often has a high moisture content, so you need to be sure your Beagle is getting all the nutrition he needs.

Homemade

There are some owners who like to prepare meals especially for their dogs – and it is probably much appreciated. The danger is that although the food is tasty, and your Beagle may enjoy the variety, you cannot be sure that it has the correct nutritional balance. If this is a route you want to go down, you will need to find out the exact ratio of fats, carbohydrates, proteins, minerals and vitamins that are needed, which is quite an undertaking.

The Barf (Biologically Appropriate Raw Food) diet is another, more natural approach to feeding. Dogs are fed a diet mimicking what they would have eaten in the wild, consisting of raw meat, bone, muscle, fat, and vegetable matter.

Beagles do well on this diet, although it is labour intensive for the owner. There are now a number of companies that specialise in producing the Barf diet in frozen form, which makes feeding this diet a lot easier.

Feeding regime

When your puppy arrives in his new home he will need four meals, evenly spaced throughout the day. This can reduce to three meals a day when he is around 12 weeks of age.

You may decide to keep to the diet recommended by your puppy's breeder, and if your pup is thriving there is no need to change. However, if your puppy is not doing well on the food, or you have problems with supply, you will need to make a change.

When switching diets, it is very important to do it on

a gradual basis, changing over from one food to the next, a little at a time, and spreading the transition over a week to 10 days. This will avoid the risk of digestive upset.

Breeds vary in the length of time they take to reach full maturity; Beagles should be considered full adults at around two years of age.

As discussed, puppies need a higher ratio of protein than adult dogs so you need to judge when is the best time to switch to an adult maintenance diet.

Protein overload can result in hyperactivity so beware of behavioural changes in your Beagle. If he is getting more calories than he is burning up, he may become difficult to manage.

When your Beagle is around six months old you can divide his rations into two meals a day, and this is a regime which should suit him for the rest of his life. Dogs thrive on routine so try to feed your Beagle at roughly the same time every day, although you don't need to become a slave to this.

There will always be times when you need to break the routine so it helps if your Beagle is adaptable, knowing that he will always get his full quota of food.

Be careful when you plan mealtimes; if a dog is exercised immediately before or after eating there

Facing page: Diet should be matched to energy output.

is a risk that he may develop a condition known as bloat. This happens when the gut twists and fills with gas which cannot escape. It is a life threatening condition and emergency surgery may be necessary. The best plan is to leave a two-hour gap either side of mealtimes before exercising your Beagle.

Fresh water

Water makes up some 70 per cent of your Beagle's bodyweight so it is essential for his health. Fresh drinking water should be readily available at all times; he will need to drink more if he is eating a dry, complete diet.

If you are travelling, always make sure you take a supply of fresh water with you.

Faddy feeders

The Beagle loves his food and is generally delighted with anything you put in his bowl. However, there are some dogs that get wise and will start refusing food if they think you are going to offer something better.

One look from those big eyes is enough to melt your heart, stirring you to greater efforts to find a food that your Beagle will really like. At first you may add some gravy, then you may try some chicken... The Beagle will quickly realise that if he holds out, tastier treats will follow.

This is a bad game to play as not only will you run out of tempting delicacies, you will also be losing your Beagle's respect.

If your Beagle is turning up his nose at mealtimes, give him 10 minutes to eat what he wants, and then take up his bowl.

Do not feed him treats in between meals, and give him fresh food at his next mealtime. If you continue this regime for a couple of days, your Beagle will realise that there is no percentage in holding out for better food as it never materialises.

In most cases, this is just a 'trying it on' phase, and if you cope with common sense, you will soon return to the status quo and your Beagle will be content with his normal rations.

If, however, your dog refuses all food for more than 24 hours you need to observe his behaviour to see if there are any signs of ill health, which may involve the need for a veterinary check up.

Bones and chews

Puppies love to chew, and many adults also enjoy gnawing on a bone. A raw marrow bone is ideal, but make sure it is always given under supervision. Nylon bones are also a favourite with Beagles.

They come in a variety of sizes and flavours, and some have raised nodules which are excellent for keeping teeth clean.

Rawhide chews are best avoided; it is all too easy for a Beagle to bite off a chunk and swallow it, with the danger of it then causing a blockage.

Ideal weight

In order to help to keep your Beagle in good health it is necessary to monitor his weight.

Because he loves his food he will always be telling you he is hungry, and in no time he will be piling on the pounds.

A dog that is carrying too much weight is vulnerable to many health issues; he has a reduced quality of life as he cannot exercise properly, and he will almost certainly have a reduced life expectancy.

When judging your Beagle's condition, look at him from above, and make sure you can see a definite waist. You should be able to feel his ribs, but not see them.

If you are concerned about your Beagle's weight, get into the habit of visiting your veterinary surgery on a monthly basis so that you can weigh him.

You can keep a record of his weight so you can make adjustments if necessary.

If you are concerned that your Beagle is putting on too much weight, or equally if you think he is underweight, consult your vet who will help you to plan a suitable diet.

Gnawing a bone or a chew provides mental stimulation.

Caring for your Beagle

The Beagle is classed as a low maintenance breed, but like all animals, he has his own special needs which you need to take on board.

Coat care

With his short coat, a Beagle needs minimal grooming – and a puppy requires even less – but do not make the mistake of ignoring this aspect of his care. A grooming session gives you the opportunity to check your dog and to discover any minor problems, such as sore places, or any abnormalities, or lumps and bumps, which may need to be investigated. Remember, if you spot a problem quickly, you increase the chance of an early diagnosis and successful treatment.

The first step is to get your puppy used to being handled so that he accepts the attention without resentment. Initially, he will wriggle and attempt to mouth you, but just ignore his protests. Hold him steady for a few moments, and reward him when he is still.

A puppy needs to learn that it is OK to be touched all over; if you fail to do this, he may try to warn you off by growling, which could develop into more problematic behaviour.

Start by handling your puppy all over, stroking him from his head to his tail. Lift up each paw in turn, and reward him with a treat when he co-operates.

Then roll him over on to his back and tickle his tummy; this is a very vulnerable position for a dog to adopt, so do not force the issue. Be firm but gentle, and give your Beagle lots of praise when he does as you ask.

When your Beagle is happy to be handled in this way, you can introduce a soft brush and spend a few minutes working on his coat, and then reward him.

He will gradually learn to accept the attention, and will relax while you groom him.

When the adult coat comes through it will be short and dense. A bristle brush is ideal for getting rid of dirt and debris and keeping the coat in good order.

Accustom your puppy to being handled from the moment he arrives.

The Beagle's coat has excellent waterproofing qualities so a quick rub-down with a towel is all your Beagle will need if he has been out in the rain.

The coat does shed, and you would be surprised how much hair can come from a short coat. When your Beagle is shedding, it will help if you groom him with a rake which will ease out the dead hair.

A rubber mitt or hound glove is also useful when the coat is shedding; it also has a massaging effect and helps to boost circulation.

Bathing

The Beagle's favourite occupation is following a scent and sometimes that involves rolling in it! Generally, you want to keep bathing to a minimum as it affects the natural oils in the coat, but at times like this you have no option but to bath your Beagle.

For this reason it is important to accustom him to the procedure from an early age so you don't have to battle with a full-grown, wriggling adult.

Make sure you use a mild moisturising shampoo specially formulated for dogs, and you can also use a conditioner which will improve the quality and appearance of the coat.

Routine care

In addition to grooming, you will need to carry out some routine care.

Eyes

Check the eyes for signs of soreness or discharge. You can use a piece of cotton wool (cotton) –a separate piece for each eye – and wipe away any debris.

Ears

Dirt and debris can collect in a Beagle's ears and because they drop down rather than being exposed to the air, they can become an ideal environment for infection. You will therefore need to check his ears on a regular basis to ensure they are clean and free from odour. You can buy specially manufactured ear wipes, or you can use a piece of cotton wool to clean them if necessary. Do not probe into the ear canal or you risk doing more harm than good.

Teeth

Dental disease is becoming more prevalent among dogs so teeth cleaning should be seen as an essential part of your care regime. The build up of tartar on the teeth can result in tooth decay, gum infection and bad breath, and if it is allowed to accumulate, you may have no option but to get the teeth cleaned under anaesthetic. When your Beagle is still a puppy, accustom him to teeth cleaning so it becomes a matter of routine. Dog toothpaste comes in a variety of meaty flavours, which your Beagle will like, so you can start by putting some toothpaste on your finger and gently rubbing his teeth. You can then progress to using a finger brush or a toothbrush, whichever you find most convenient Remember to reward your Beagle when he co-operates and then he will positively look forward to his teeth-cleaning sessions.

Nails

Nail trimming is a task dreaded by many owners, and many dogs, but if you start early on, your Beagle will get used to the task you have to perform and will not fight against it. Most Beagles have white nails so you will be able to see the quick (the vein that runs through the nail), which you must avoid at all costs. If you cut the quick it will bleed profusely and cause considerable discomfort. The best policy is to trim little and often so the nails don't grow too long, and you do not risk cutting too much and catching the quick. If you are worried about trimming your Beagle's nails, go to your vet so you can see it done properly. If you are still concerned, you can always use the services of a professional groomer.

Regular brushing removes dirt from the coat.

Clean the ears when necessary.

In addition to brushing, you can use a tooth scaler to remove tartar from the teeth.

Show preparation

If you want to exhibit your Beagle in the show ring, he needs to look his very best. He needs to be clean so you will probably need to bath him prior to the show. A good-quality conditioner will improve the condition of his coat, but do not bath your dog the day before a show as this will affect the natural oils in his coat. A brush with a bristle brush and a polish with a chamois leather is all you need to do to the coat before you go into the ring. Some exhibitors use a rake around the neck area to reduce the amount of coat. This enhances the outline and stops the neck from looking scruffy. There is also a growing tendency to trim the underside of the tail, but as the Breed Standard specifically asks for a tail that is "well covered with hair" – a "brush tail" according to the American Standard – this can be a perilous route to go down.

Exercise

The Beagle was bred to run, and so exercise is an important component of his physical and mental wellbeing. However, do not get carried away with taking your puppy on long route marches.

Over-exercise can damage growing bones and joints so in the first few weeks your Beagle will get as much exercise as he needs playing in the garden.

Facing page: This is an active breed that needs to run.

You can also practise lead-walking so your puppy is ready to be taken out and about when he has completed his vaccination programme.

Free running exercise is a delight for Beagles – but you need to bear in mind that a scenthound can become deaf to your calls when he finds a particularly interesting smell. He will be so busy tracking the scent that he becomes oblivious to everything else. This can lead him into all sorts off trouble – and if the scent path takes him across a road, the consequences could be fatal.

It is important to practise your recall, but you also need to find safe areas to exercise your Beagle. If in doubt, keep him on an extending lead; he will still have the opportunity to investigate scents – but you will remain in control.

The older Beagle

We are fortunate that the Beagle has a good life expectancy – most will get to early teens and some may even do better.

As your Beagle grows older, he may sleep more and he may be reluctant to go for longer walks. He may show signs of stiffness when he gets up from his bed, but these generally ease when he starts moving.

Some older Beagles may have impaired vision, and some may become a little deaf, but as long as their senses do not deteriorate dramatically, this is something older dogs learn to live with.

If you treat your older dog with kindness and consideration, he will enjoy his later years and suffer the minimum of discomfort.

It is advisable to switch him over to a senior diet, which is more suited to his needs, and you may need to adjust the quantity, as he will not be burning up the calories as he did when he was younger and more energetic.

The older Beagle will often prefer a softer diet, and you will need to keep a close check on his teeth as these may cause problems. Make sure his sleeping quarters are warm and free from draughts, and if he gets wet, make sure you dry him thoroughly. Most important of all, be guided by your Beagle.

He will have good days when he feels up to going for a walk, and other days when he would prefer to potter in the garden. If you have a younger dog at home, this may well stimulate your Beagle to take more of an interest in what is going on.

However, you need to make sure he is not pestered as he needs to rest undisturbed when he is tired.

Letting go

Inevitably there comes a time when your Beagle is not enjoying a good quality of life, and you need to make the painful decision to let him go.

We would all wish that our dogs died, painlessly, in their sleep but, unfortunately, this is rarely the case.

However, we can allow our dogs to die with dignity, and to suffer as a little as possible, and this should be our way of saying thank you for the wonderful companionship they have given us.

When you feel the time is drawing close, talk to your vet who will be able to make an objective assessment of your Beagle's condition and will help you to make the right decision.

This is the hardest thing you will ever have to do as a dog owner, and it is only natural to grieve for your beloved Beagle. But eventually you will be able to look back on the happy memories of times spent together, and this will bring much comfort.

You may, in time, feel that your life is not complete without a Beagle, and you will feel ready to welcome a new puppy into your home.

Facing page: You will have many happy memories to look back on...

Social skills

To live in the modern world, without fears and anxieties, your Beagle needs to receive an education in social skills so that he learns to cope calmly and confidently in a wide variety of situations. The Beagle is an outgoing dog, with few hang-ups, and will relish the opportunity to broaden his horizons.

Early learning

The breeder will have begun a programme of socialization by getting the puppies used to all the sights and sounds of a busy household. You need to continue this when your pup arrives in his new home, making sure he is not worried by household equipment, such the vacuum cleaner or the washing machine, and that he gets used to unexpected noises from the radio and television.

To begin with, your puppy needs to get used to all the members of his new family, but then you should give him the opportunity to meet friends and other people who visit your home.

If you do not have children, make sure your puppy has the chance to meet and play with other people's children, making sure interactions are always supervised, so he learns that people come in small sizes, too. The Beagle is a sociable dog and enjoys the comings and goings of a busy household so meeting and greeting will rarely be a problem. However, he can be pushy when it comes to getting attention and he may start demanding it by jumping up or barking. If you think your Beagle is attempting to rule the roost, you need to withdraw your focus and only give him attention when he is quiet and has all four feet on the ground.

- If your Beagle jumps up at you, demanding attention (possibly pushing other dogs out of the way), simply ignore him. Turn away and do not speak to him, even to tell him off, as he will regard this as another form of attention. Adopt the same procedure if he starts to bark.

- Wait until he is calm and quiet, with all four feet on the ground, and then give him the attention he craves. You will need to be completely consistent in your training and repeat this lesson continually so that your Beagle learns that his attention-seeking strategies do not work. He will only get attention when you are ready to give it.

It is so easy to give in to the high-spirited Beagle thinking that his behaviour is just a minor nuisance. But it doesn't work like that; if a dog thinks his behaviour is OK he will not only repeat it, he will escalate it – and then you are in real trouble.

The outside world

When your puppy has completed his vaccinations, he is ready to venture into the outside world. Beagles are generally pretty confident but there is a lot for a youngster to take on board, so do not swamp him with too many new experiences when you first set out.

Obviously you need to work at lead-training before you set out on your first expedition. There will be plenty of distractions to cope with, so you do not want additional problems of coping with a dog that is pulling or lagging on the lead.

Hopefully, you can set off with your Beagle walking by your side on a loose lead. He may need additional encouragement when you venture further afield so arm yourself with some extra special treats, which will give him a good reason to focus on you when required!

Start socialising your puppy in a quiet area with light traffic, and only progress to a busier place when he is ready. There is so much to see and hear – people (maybe carrying bags or umbrellas), pushchairs, bicycles, cars, lorries, machinery – so give your puppy a chance to take it all in.

If he does appear worried, do not fall into the trap of sympathising with him which will make him think there is good reason for his concern. Equally do not force him to confront the thing that is worrying him as he may panic fearing there is no escape.

Instead, give him a little space so he feels he is out of the 'danger zone' and distract him with a few treats. Then encourage him to walk past, using an encouraging tone of voice, never forcing him by pulling or yanking on the lead.

Facing page: Plan meetings with dogs who are sound in temperament.

Reward him for any forward movement, and your puppy will soon learn that he can trust you, and there is nothing to fear.

Your pup also needs to continue his education in canine manners, stared by his mother and by his littermates, as he needs to be able to greet all dogs calmly, giving the signals that say he is friendly and offers no threat.

The Beagle is an outgoing dog and is nearly always friendly in his intentions, but it never hurts to take extra care.

If you have a friend who has a dog of sound temperament, this is an ideal way to get your puppy used to social interactions. As he gets older and more established, you can widen his circle of canine acquaintances.

Training classes

A training class will give your Beagle the opportunity to work alongside other dogs in a controlled situation, and he will also learn to focus on you in a different, distracting environment.

Both these lessons will be vital as your dog matures.

However, the training class needs to be of the highest calibre or you risk doing more harm than good. Before you go along with your puppy, attend a class as an observer to make sure you are happy with what goes on.

Find out the following:

- How much training experience do the instructors have?

- Are the classes divided into appropriate age categories?

- Do the instructors have experience training Beagles?

- Do they use positive, reward-based training methods?

If the training class is well run, it is certainly worth attending. Both you and your Beagle will learn useful training exercises; it will increase his social skills, and you will have the chance to talk to lots of like-minded dog enthusiasts.

Training
guidelines

The Beagle is an intelligent dog and he enjoys co-operating with his human family. However, he has a stubborn streak which can get in the way of training. You need to work hard at motivating him so he always wants to please you...

You will be keen to get started, but in your rush to get training underway, do not neglect the fundamentals which could make the difference between success and failure.

You need to get into the mindset of a Beagle, encouraging the behaviour you want and avoiding confrontation so he doesn't switch off. Decide on your priorities for training, and then think of ways of making your training as much fun – and as positive – as possible.

When you start training, try to observe the following guidelines:

Choose an area that is free from distractions so your puppy will focus on you. You can move on to a more challenging environment as your pup progresses.

Do not train your puppy just after he has eaten or when you have returned from exercise. He will either be too full, or too tired, to concentrate.

Do not train if you are in a bad mood, or if you are short of time. These sessions always end in disaster!

Providing a worthwhile reward is an essential tool in training. This is not difficult with a Beagle who has a high regard for food, although there are some Beagles who prefer to work for a favourite toy.

If you decide to use a toy, make sure it is only brought out for training sessions so that it accrues added value.

Keep your verbal cues simple, and always use the same one for each exercise. For example, when you ask your puppy to go into the Down position, the cue is Down, not Lie Down, Get Down, or anything else.

Remember, your Beagle does not speak English; he associates the sound of the word with the action.

If your dog is finding an exercise difficult, break it down into small steps so it is easier to understand. This may be the time to bring out some extra special treats to motivate your Beagle.

Do not make your training sessions boring and repetitious; your Beagle will lose concentration and will cease to co-operate.

Do not train for too long, particularly with a young puppy, who has a very short attention span, and always end training sessions on a positive note.

This does not necessarily mean getting an exercise right. If your pup is tired and making mistakes, ask him to do a simple exercise so you have the opportunity to praise and reward him.

You may well find that he benefits from having a break and will make better progress next time you try.

Above all, make training fun so you and your Beagle enjoy spending quality time together.

First lessons

Like all puppies, a young Beagle will soak up new experiences like a sponge, so training should start from the time your pup arrives in his new home.

Wearing a collar

You may, or may not, want your Beagle to wear a collar all the time. But when he goes out in public places he will need to be on a lead, and so he should be used to the feel of a collar around his neck.

The best plan is to accustom your pup to wearing a soft collar for a few minutes at a time until he gets used to it.

Fit the collar so that you can get at least two fingers between the collar and his neck. Then have a game to distract his attention.

This will work for a few moments; then he will stop, put his back leg up behind his neck and scratch away at the peculiar itchy thing which feels so odd.

Bend down, rotate the collar, pat him on the head

and distract him by playing with a toy or giving him a treat.

Once he has worn the collar for a few minutes each day, he will soon ignore it and become used to it.

Remember, never leave the collar on the puppy unsupervised, especially when he is outside in the garden, or when he is in his crate, as it is could get snagged, causing serious injury.

Walking on the lead

This is a simple exercise, but Beagles can get into the habit of pulling ahead, particularly if you are en route to a favourite exercise area. You need to get on top of this before pulling becomes an ingrained habit.

The best plan is to arm yourself with some extra special treats and reward your Beagle the moment he is walking beside you on a loose lead. In this way, he is left in no doubt that a slack lead equals a mouth-watering reward.

Once your puppy is used to the collar, take him outside into your secure garden where there are no distractions.

Attach the lead and, to begin with, allow him to wander with the lead trailing, making sure it does not become snagged. Then pick up the lead and follow the pup where he wants to go; he needs to get used to the sensation of being attached to you.

The next stage is to get your Beagle to follow you, and for this you will need some treats.

To give yourself the best chance of success, make sure the treats are high value – cheese, sausage or cooked liver – so your Beagle is motivated to work with you.

Show him you have a treat in your hand, and then encourage him to follow you.

Walk a few paces, and if he is walking with you, stop and reward him. If he puts on the brakes, simply change direction and lure him with the treat.

Next, introduce some changes of direction so your puppy is walking confidently alongside you. At this stage, introduce a verbal cue – "heel" – when your puppy is in the correct position.

You can then graduate to walking your puppy outside the home, as long as he has completed his vaccination programme, starting in quiet areas and building up to busier environments.

Training strategy

Some Beagles decide that pulling on the lead is a good option, and, in no time, the dog is taking you for a walk. This soon becomes an unpleasant experience, so it is important to adopt a strategy that makes your Beagle realise there is absolutely no percentage in pulling.

Restrict lead training to the garden in the initial stages so you are working in an environment that is free from distractions.

Walk a few paces, being very aware of any tension on the lead. If you feel the lead tighten and your Beagle is attempting to get ahead of you, stop, change direction, and set off again.

Your Beagle needs to understand that pulling ahead has exactly the opposite effect to the one he wants. Rather than calling the tune, he has to co-operate with you.

Keep a good supply of tasty treats and remember only reward – with food and with verbal praise – when he is walking on a loose lead by your side. The mistake made by many owners at this stage is to use the treats to lure the dog into position rather than rewarding him for the correct behaviour.

• Keep training sessions short, and when you are ready to venture into the outside world, do not be too ambitious to begin with. Build up the level of distraction and the duration of lead walking only when your Beagle is consistently showing the behaviour you want.

Remember, your puppy has a very short attention span...

Come when called

The Beagle is a hound at heart and when he catches wind of an interesting scent, he simply cannot resist it. For this reason free running exercise needs to be restricted to safe, preferably enclosed, areas where there is no chance of your Beagle getting into trouble.

However, this does not mean that you should neglect recall training; you still need your dog to come back to you even if his freedom is restricted – and there may be an emergency when a response to the recall could save your Beagle's life.

Hopefully, the breeder will have laid the foundations simply by calling the puppies to "come" when it is dinnertime, or when they are moving from one place to another.

You can build on this when your puppy arrives in his new home, asking him to "come" when he is in a confined space, such as the kitchen. This is a good place to build up a positive association with the verbal cue – particularly if you ask your puppy to "come" to get his dinner!

The next stage is to transfer the lesson to the garden. Arm yourself with some treats, and wait until your puppy is distracted. Then call him, using a higher-pitched, excited tone of voice. At this stage, a puppy wants to be with you, so capitalize on this and keep practising the verbal cue, and rewarding your puppy with a treat and lots of praise when he comes to you.

Now you are ready to introduce some distractions. Try calling him when someone else is in the garden, or wait a few minutes until he is investigating a really interesting scent. When he responds, make a really big fuss of him and give him extra treats so he knows it is worth his while to come to you. If your puppy responds, immediately reward him with a treat.

If he is slow to come, run away a few steps and then call again, making yourself sound really exciting. Jump up and down, open your arms wide to welcome him; it doesn't matter how silly you look, he needs to see you as the most fun person in the world.

When you have a reliable recall in the garden, you can venture into the outside world. Do not be too ambitious to begin with; try a recall in a quiet place with the minimum of distractions so you can be more certain of success.

Do not make the mistake of only asking your dog to come at the end of his allotted exercise period. What is the incentive in coming back to you if all you do is clip on his lead, marking the end of his free time? Instead, call your dog at random times, giving him a treat and a stroke, and then letting him go free again. In this way, coming to you – and focusing on you – is always rewarding.

Coming back must always be the most rewarding option.

Stationary exercises

The Sit and Down are easy to teach, and mastering these exercises will be rewarding for both you and your Beagle. The Beagle can be exuberant, particularly when he is growing up, so it is useful to have a means of bringing proceedings to a standstill before everyone gets carried away!

Sit

The best method is to lure your Beagle into position, and for this you can use a treat or his food bowl. Hold the reward (a treat or food bowl) above his head. As he looks up, he will lower his hindquarters and go into a sit. Practise this a few times and when your puppy understands what you are asking, introduce the verbal cue, "sit".

When your Beagle understands the exercise, he will

respond to the verbal cue alone, and you will not need to reward him every time he sits.

However, it is a good idea to give him a treat on a random basis when he co-operates to keep him guessing!

Down

This is an important lesson, and can be a lifesaver if an emergency arises and you need to bring your Beagle to an instant halt.

You can start with your dog in a sit or a stand for this exercise. Stand or kneel in front of him and show him you have a treat in your hand.

Hold the treat just in front of his nose and slowly lower it towards the ground, between his front legs.

As your Beagle follows the treat he will go down on his front legs and, in a few moments, his hindquarters will follow.

Close your hand over the treat so he doesn't cheat and get the treat before he is in the correct position. As soon as he is in the Down, give him the treat and lots of praise.

Keep practising, and when your Beagle understands what you want, introduce the verbal cue, "down".

When your Beagle has learnt an exercise, take it to new places so he learns to generalise.

Control exercises

These exercises are not the most exciting, but they are important in establishing a relationship of mutual respect with your Beagle.

Wait

This exercise teaches your Beagle to wait in position until you give the next command; it differs from the stay exercise where he must stay where you have left him for a more prolonged period.

The most useful application of 'wait' is when you are getting your dog out of the car and you need him to stay in position until you clip on his lead.

Start with your puppy on the lead to give you a greater chance of success. Ask him to sit, and stand in front him. Step back one pace, holding your hand, palm flat, facing him. Wait a second and then come back to stand in front of him. You can then reward

him and release him with a word, such as "OK".

Practise this a few times, waiting a little longer before you reward him, and then introduce the verbal cue, "wait".

You can reinforce the lesson by using it in different situations, such as asking your Beagle to "wait" before you put his food bowl down.

Stay

You need to differentiate this exercise from the Wait by using a different hand signal and a different verbal cue.

Start with your Beagle in the down as he is most likely to be secure in this position. Stand by his side and then step forwards, with your hand held back, palm facing the dog.

Step back, release him, and then reward him. Practice until your Beagle understands the exercise and then introduce the verbal cue, "stay".

Gradually increase the distance you can leave your puppy, and increase the challenge by walking around him – and even stepping over him – so that he learns he must stay until you release him.

Leave/off

A response to this verbal cue means that your Beagle will learn to give up a toy on request, and it follows on that he will give up anything when he is asked, which is very useful if he has got hold of a forbidden object.

You can use the same basic training strategy if you want your Beagle to get off the sofa or your favourite armchair.

The Beagle is unlikely to become possessive over his toys but he may attempt to take liberties and get on the furniture – and then he may be difficult to budge. The aim in both scenarios is to encourage co-operation but to avoid confrontation.

Leave

The Leave command can be taught quite easily when you are first playing with your puppy.

As you, gently, take a toy from his mouth, introduce the verbal cue, "leave", and then praise him. If he is reluctant, swap the toy for another toy or a treat. This will usually do the trick.

Do not try to pull the toy from his mouth if he refuses to give it up, as you will make the situation confrontational.

Let the toy go dead in your hand, and then swap it for a new toy, or a really high-value treat, so this becomes the better option.

Off

The verbal cue, "off" can be taught before you need it! If your Beagle is in his bed or at the top of a couple of steps, lure him with a treat and when he moves, reward him.

When he understands what you want, introduce the verbal cue, "off". Soon he will respond to this without needing a lure. If you find your Beagle in a 'forbidden' place, such as on your bed, you do not need to reprimand him and risk a stand-off.

Simply give him his verbal cue, "off" and he will co-operate because he knows a reward will follow. Remember to make a big fuss of your Beagle when he does as you ask.

Being in your good books means a lot to a Beagle so never stint on giving him verbal praise and telling him he is the best dog in the world!

Facing page: If you use positive, reward based training, your Beagle will be happy to co-operate.

Opportunities for Beagles

The Beagle has a brain and he will relish the opportunity to use it. However, his instinct to scent and track will always be at the forefront of his mind. Training must be geared to motivating your Beagle and setting realistic expectations. Have fun with your Beagle, channel his considerable intelligence and who knows what you will achieve?

Good Citizen Scheme

The Kennel Club Good Citizen Scheme was introduced to promote responsible dog ownership, and to teach dogs basic good manners. In the US there is one test; in the UK there are four award levels: Puppy Foundation, Bronze, Silver and Gold.

Exercises within the scheme include:

- Walking on lead
- Road walking
- Control at door/gate
- Food manners

- Recall

- Stay

- Send to bed

- Emergency stop

Obedience

If your Beagle has mastered basic obedience, you may want to get involved in competitive obedience. The exercises include: heelwork at varying paces, with dog and handler following a pattern decided by the judge, stays, recalls, retrieves, sendaways, scent discrimination and distance control. The exercises get progressively harder as you progress up the classes.

A Beagle will readily learn the exercises that are used in obedience competitions, but this is a discipline that calls for a very high degree of precision and accuracy which does not suit all dogs, or all handlers.

Rally O

If you do not want to get involved in the rigours of Competitive Obedience, you may find that a sport called Rally O is more to your liking.

This is loosely based on Obedience, and also has

a few exercises borrowed from Agility (see below) when you get to the highest levels. Handler and dog must complete a course, in the designated order, which has a variety of up to 20 different exercises. The course is timed and the team must complete within the time limit that is set, but there are no bonus marks for speed.

The great advantage of Rally O is that it is very relaxed, and anyone can compete; indeed, it has proved very popular for handlers with disabilities, as they are able to work their dogs to a high standard and compete on equal terms with other competitors.

Agility

The Beagle has an athletic build and will have no problems negotiating the obstacles that make up an agility course.

However, you need a good element of control with this sport as the dog works off-lead. In most cases, the course is laid out in a field and so there will be plenty of enticing sniffs on offer.

You need to get your Beagle working for a high value reward, such as extra special treats or a favourite toy, which he finds even more rewarding than those tempting smells...

In competition, each dog completes the course

individually and is assessed on both time and accuracy. The dog that completes the course in the fastest time, with the fewest faults, wins the class. The obstacles include an A-frame, a dog-walk, weaving poles, a see-saw, tunnels, and jumps.

Showing

Exhibiting a dog in the show ring sounds easy but, in fact, it entails a lot of training and preparation, particularly when you are asking a strong-minded, heavyweight breed to compete in a beauty competition.

Your Beagle needs to be calm and confident in the busy show atmosphere, so you need to work on his socialisation, and also take him to ringcraft classes so you both learn what is required in the ring.

A Beagle needs to be trained to show himself to best advantage in the ring.

Your Beagle will be subjected to a detailed hands-on examination by the judge; he must learn to stand still in a show pose and to move on a loose lead so the judge can assess his gait. Showing at the top level is highly addictive, so watch out, once you start, you will never have a free date in your diary!

Dancing with dogs

This is a relatively new discipline that is growing in popularity despite the hard work that is involved. Perhaps surprisingly, the Beagle has a special liking for this sport and a number of Beagles have been highly successful. Dog and handler must perform a choreographed routine to music, allowing the dog to perform an array of tricks and moves which delight the crowd.

There are two categories: heelwork to music, where the dog stays close to his handler in a variety of heelwork positions and canine freestyle, where the dog works at a greater distance and performs some of the more spectacular moves.

A panel of judges mark the routine for content, accuracy and musical interpretation. Both categories demand a huge amount of training but if you keep training sessions light-hearted, with plenty of tasty treats on offer, the Beagle will prove to be a real crowd-pleaser!

Facing page: The Beagle has made his mark as a dancing dog.

Health care

We are fortunate that the Beagle is a healthy breed and, with good routine care, a well-balanced diet, and sufficient exercise, most will experience few health problems.

However, it is your responsibility to put a programme of preventative health care in place, and this should start from the moment your puppy, or older dog, arrives in his new home.

Vaccinations

Dogs are subject to a number of contagious diseases. In the old days, these were killers, and resulted in heartbreak for many owners. Vaccinations have now been developed, and the occurrence of the major infectious diseases is now very rare. However, this will only remain the case if all pet owners follow a strict policy of vaccinating their dogs.

There are vaccinations available for the following diseases:

Adenovirus (Canine Adenovirus): This attacks the liver and affected dogs have a classic 'blue eye'.

Distemper: A viral disease which causes chest and gastro-intestinal damage. The brain may also be affected, leading to fits and paralysis.

Parvovirus: Causes severe gastro enteritis, and most commonly affects puppies.

Leptospirosis: This bacterial disease is carried by rats and affects many mammals, including humans. It causes liver and kidney damage.

Rabies: A virus that affects the nervous system and is invariably fatal. The first signs are abnormal behavior when the infected dog may bite another animal or a person. Paralysis and death follow. Vaccination is compulsory in most countries. In the UK, dogs travelling overseas must be vaccinated.

Kennel cough: There are several strains of kennel cough, but they all result in a harsh, dry, cough. This disease is rarely fatal; in fact most dogs make a good recovery within a matter of weeks and show few signs of ill health while they are affected. However, kennel cough is highly infectious among dogs that live together so, for this reason, most boarding kennels will insist that your dog is protected by the vaccine, which is given as nose drops.

Lyme disease: This is a bacterial disease transmitted by ticks. The first signs are limping, but the heart, kidneys and nervous system can also be affected. The ticks that transmit the disease occur in specific regions, such as the north-east states of the USA, some of the southern states, California and the upper Mississippi region. Lyme disease is still rare in the UK so vaccinations are not routinely offered.

Vaccination programme

In the USA, the American Animal Hospital Association advises vaccination for core diseases, which they list as distemper, adenovirus, parvovirus and rabies. The requirement for vaccinating for non-core diseases – leptospriosis, lyme disease and kennel cough – should be assessed depending on a dog's individual risk and his likely exposure to the disease.

In the UK, vaccinations are routinely given for distemper, adenovirus, leptospirosis and parvovirus.

In most cases, a puppy will start his vaccinations at around eight weeks of age, with the second part given a fortnight later. However, this does vary depending on the individual policy of veterinary practices, and the incidence of disease in your area. You should also talk to your vet about whether to give annual booster vaccinations. This depends on an individual dog's levels of immunity, and how long a particular vaccine remains effective.

Parasites

No matter how well you look after your Beagle, you will have to accept that parasites (internal and external) are ever present, and you need to take preventative action.

Internal parasites: As the name suggests, these parasites live inside your dog. Most will find a home in the digestive tract, but there is also a parasite that lives in the heart. If infestation is unchecked, a dog's health will be severely jeopardised, but routine preventative treatment is simple and effective.

External parasites: These parasites live on your dog's body – in his skin and fur, and sometimes in his ears.

Roundworm

This is found in the small intestine, and signs of infestation will be a poor coat, a pot belly, diarrhoea and lethargy. Pregnant mothers should be treated, but it is almost inevitable that parasites will be passed on to the puppies.

For this reason, a breeder will start a worming

programme, which you will need to continue.

Ask your vet for advice on treatment, which will be ongoing throughout your dog's life.

Tapeworm

Infection occurs when fleas and lice are ingested; the adult worm takes up residence in the small intestine, releasing mobile segments (which contain eggs) that can be seen in a dog's faeces as small rice-like grains.

The only other obvious sign of infestation is irritation of the anus. Again, routine preventative treatment is required throughout your Beagle's life.

Heartworm

This parasite is transmitted by mosquitoes, and so will only occur where these insects thrive. A warm environment is needed for the parasite to develop, so it is more likely to be present in areas with a warm, humid climate.

However, it is found in all parts of the USA, although its prevalence does vary. At present, heartworm is rarely seen in the UK.

Heartworm live in the right side of the heart. Larvae can grow up to 14 inches (35.5cm) in length.

A dog with heartworm is at severe risk from heart failure, so preventative treatment, as advised by your vet, is essential. Dogs living in the USA should have regular blood tests to check for the presence of infection.

Lungworm

Lungworm, or *Angiostrongylus vasorum*, is a parasite that lives in the heart and major blood vessels supplying the lungs. It can cause many problems, such as breathing difficulties, blood-clotting problems, sickness and diarrhoea, seizures, and can be fatal.

The parasite is carried by slugs and snails, and the

dog becomes infected when ingesting these, often accidentally when rummaging through undergrowth. Lungworm is not common, but it is on the increase and a responsible owner should be aware of it.

Fortunately, it is easily preventable and even affected dogs usually make a full recovery if treated early enough. Your vet will be able to advise you on the risks in your area and what form of treatment may be required.

Fleas

A dog may carry dog fleas, cat fleas, and even human fleas. The flea stays on the dog only long enough to have a blood meal and to breed, but its presence will result in itching and scratching. If your dog has an allergy to fleas, which is usually a reaction to the flea's saliva, he will scratch himself until he is raw.

Preventative treatment, which may be in the form of spot on treatment, tablets, insecticidal spray or shampoo should be administered on a routine basis. Ask your vet which is the most effective treatment to use, depending on your locality.

Bear in mind that the whole environment your dog lives in will need to be sprayed, and all other pets living in your home will also need to be treated.

How to detect fleas

You may suspect your dog has fleas, but how can you be sure? There are two methods to try.

Run a fine comb through your dog's coat, and see if you can detect the presence of fleas on the skin, or clinging to the comb. Alternatively, sit your dog on white paper and rub his back. This will dislodge faeces from the fleas, which will be visible as small brown specks. To double check, shake the specks on to damp cotton-wool (cotton). Flea faeces consists of the dried blood taken from the host, so if the specks turn a lighter shade of red, you know your dog has fleas.

Ticks

These are blood-sucking parasites which are most frequently found in rural areas where sheep or deer are present. The main danger is their ability to pass lyme disease to both dogs and humans.

Lyme disease is prevalent in some areas of the USA, although it is still rare in the UK. The treatment you give your dog for fleas generally works for ticks, but you should discuss the best product to use with your vet.

How to remove a tick

If you spot a tick on your dog, do not try to pluck it off as you risk leaving the hard mouth parts embedded in his skin The best way to remove a tick is to use a fine pair of tweezers, or you can buy a tick remover. Grasp the tick head firmly and then pull the tick straight out from the skin. If you are using a tick remover, check the instructions, as some recommend a circular twist when pulling. When you have removed the tick, clean the area with mild soap and water.

Ear mites

These parasites live in the outer ear canal. The signs of infestation are a brown, waxy discharge, and your dog will continually shake his head and scratch his ear.

If you suspect your Beagle has ear mites, a visit to the vet will be needed so that medicated ear drops can be prescribed.

Fur mites

These small, white parasites are visible to the naked eye and are often referred to as 'walking dandruff'.

They cause a scurfy coat and mild itchiness. However, they are zoonetic – transferable to humans

– so prompt treatment with an insecticide prescribed by your vet is essential.

Harvest mites

These are picked up from the undergrowth, and can be seen as a bright orange patch on the webbing between the toes, although this can be found elsewhere on the body, such as on the ear flaps.

Treatment is effective with the appropriate insecticide.

Skin mites

There are two types of parasite that burrow into a dog's skin.

Demodex canis is transferred from a mother to her pups while they are feeding. Treatment is with a topical preparation, and sometimes antibiotics are needed.

The other skin mite is *Sarcoptes scabiei*, causes intense itching and hair loss. It is highly contagious, so all dogs in a household will need to be treated, which involves repeated bathing with a medicated shampoo.

Common
ailments

As with all living animals, dogs can be affected by a variety of ailments. Most can be treated effectively after consulting with your vet, who will prescribe appropriate medication and will advise you on how to care for your dog's needs.

Here are some of the more common problems that could affect your Beagle, with advice on how to deal with them.

Anal glands

These are two small sacs on either side of the anus, which produce a dark-brown secretion that dogs use when they mark their territory. The anal glands should empty every time a dog defecates but if they become blocked or impacted, a dog will experience increasing discomfort. He may nibble at his rear end,

or scoot his bottom along the ground to relieve the irritation.

Treatment involves a trip to the vet, who will empty the glands manually. It is important to do this without delay or infection may occur.

Dental problems

Good dental hygiene will do much to minimise gum infection and tooth decay, which is why teeth cleaning should be part of your regular care routine. If tartar accumulates to the extent that you cannot remove it by brushing, the vet will need to intervene. In a situation such as this, an anaesthetic will need to be administered so the tartar can be removed manually.

Diarrhoea

There are many reasons why a dog has diarrhoea, but most commonly it is the result of scavenging, a sudden change of diet, or an adverse reaction to a particular type of food.

If your dog is suffering from diarrhoea, the first step is to withdraw food for a day. It is important that he does not dehydrate, so make sure that fresh drinking water is available.

However, drinking too much can increase the

diarrhoea, which may be accompanied by vomiting, so limit how much he drinks at any one time.

After allowing the stomach to rest, feed a bland diet, such as white fish or chicken with boiled rice, for a few days. In most cases, your dog's motions will return to normal and you can resume usual feeding, although this should be done gradually.

However, if this fails to work and the diarrhoea persists for more than a few days, you should consult you vet.

Your dog may have an infection which needs to be treated with antibiotics, or the diarrhoea may indicate some other problem which needs expert diagnosis.

Ear infections

The Beagle has drop ears which means that air does not circulate freely as it does with prick-eared dogs. This means that the Beagle is more vulnerable to ear infections.

A healthy ear is clean with no sign of redness or inflammation, and no evidence of a waxy brown discharge or a foul odour. If you see your dog scratching his ear, shaking his head, or holding one ear at an odd angle, you will need to consult your vet.

The most likely causes are ear mites, an infection, or there may be a foreign body, such as a grass seed, trapped in the ear.

Depending on the cause, treatment is with medicated ear drops, possibly containing antibiotics. If a foreign body is suspected, the vet will need to carry out further investigations.

Eye problems

The Beagle's eyes are large and set well apart. They should not be sunken nor prominent, which means that they should not be predisposed to infection or vulnerable to injury or trauma, which is the case with breeds such as the Pekingese, which have somewhat bulging eyes.

If your Beagle's eyes look red and sore, he may be suffering from conjunctivitis. This may, or may not be accompanied with a watery or a crusty discharge. Conjunctivitis can be caused by a bacterial or viral infection, it could be the result of an injury, or it could be an adverse reaction to pollen.

You will need to consult your vet for a correct diagnosis, but in the case of an infection, treatment with medicated eye drops is effective. Conjunctivitis may also be the first sign of more serious inherited eye problems (see Breed-specific disorders)

Foreign bodies

In the home, puppies – and some older dogs
– cannot resist chewing anything that looks
interesting.

The toys you choose for your dog should be suitably
robust to withstand damage, but children's toys
can be irresistible. Some dogs will chew
– and swallow – anything from socks,
tights, and any other items from the
laundry basket to golf balls and
stones from the garden.

Obviously, these items are indigestible and could cause an obstruction in your dog's intestine, which is potentially lethal.

The signs to look for are vomiting, and a tucked up posture. The dog will often be restless and will look as though he is in pain. In this situation, you must get your dog to the vet without delay, as surgery may be needed to remove the obstruction.

Foreign bodies in the form of seeds and grass awns can also cause problems so it is important to inspect your Beagle thoroughly if he has been exercising in long grass or in fields where crops are growing.

Heatstroke

The Beagle, with his short coat, is not prone to over-heating. In common with all the scent hounds, he has a large nose with well-developed nostrils which makes for an efficient respiratory system unlike some breeds, such as Boxers or Pekingese, which have flat, up-turned noses and may suffer from breathing problems.

However, you should never take risks with your Beagle. If the weather is warm, make sure he has access to shady areas, and wait for a cooler part of the day before going for a walk. Be extra careful if you leave your Beagle in the car as the temperature

can rise dramatically – even on a cloudy day. Heatstroke can happen very rapidly, and unless you are able to lower your dog's temperature, it can be fatal.

If your dog appears to be suffering from heatstroke, lie him flat and work at lowering his temperature by spraying him with cool water and covering him with wet towels. As soon as he has made some recovery, take him to the vet, where cold intravenous fluids can be administered.

Lameness/limping

There are a wide variety of reasons why a dog can go lame, from a simple muscle strain, to a fracture, ligament damage, or more complex problems with the joints. If you are concerned about your dog, do not delay in seeking help.

As your Beagle becomes more elderly, he may suffer from arthritis, which you will see as general stiffness, particularly when he gets up after resting.

It will help if you ensure his bed is in a warm draught-free location, and if your Beagle gets wet after exercise, you must dry him thoroughly.

If your Beagle seems to be in pain, consult your vet who will be able to help with pain relief medication.

Skin problems

If your dog is scratching or nibbling at his skin, first check he is free from fleas. There are other external parasites which cause itching and hair loss, but you will need a vet to help you find the culprit.

An allergic reaction is another major cause of skin problems.

It can be quite an undertaking to find the cause of the allergy, and you will need to follow your vet's advice, which often requires eliminating specific ingredients from the diet, as well as looking at environmental factors.

Breed-specific disorders

Like all pedigree dogs, the Beagle does have some breed-related disorders. If diagnosed with any of the diseases listed here, it is important to remember that they can affect offspring so breeding from such dogs should be discouraged.

There are now recognised screening tests to enable breeders to check for affected individuals and hence reduce the prevalence of these diseases within the breed.

DNA testing is also becoming more widely available, and as research into the different genetic diseases progresses, more DNA tests are being developed.

Atopic dermatitis

This condition, which is seen as intense itching usually involving the face, paws and underparts, is the result of an allergic reaction.

The cause is hard to detect; it may be the result of fleas or inhaling allergens such as dust mites or pollen. The Beagle seems predisposed to this condition, which can only be resolved by eliminating all possible causes and then seeking appropriate treatment.

Cherry eye

This is caused by a prolapse of the gland that lies beneath the third eyelid, which is known asthe nictitans gland. Sometimes the gland protrudes over the edge of the eyelid and appears as a pink, fleshy mass. Surgery, if performed soon after the prolapse, is effective and should prevent a recurrence of the problem.

Epilepsy

This condition involves seizures which may be partial, affecting only one leg, or they may affect the whole body and the dog may temporarily lose consciousness.

A dog may have single fits or he may fit continually over a period of time. Medication is available to control the fits but there is no known cure. It is important to research bloodlines for the incidence of epilepsy before selecting breeding stock.

Hip dysplasia

This is where the hip joint has not formed correctly and fails to conform to the ball and socket structure which allows ease of movement. The condition is first seen as stiffness in the joints and may be detected while a Beagle is growing.

Surgery can be effective but it is likely that arthritis will develop in the affected joint. Prospective breeding stock should be hip-scored and only the dogs with the best scores should be selected for breeding.

Hypothyroidism

Caused by an under-active thyroid gland, an affected Beagle will be lethargic, prone to weight gain and will have a poor coat as, effectively, his whole metabolism is slowed down. The condition requires lifelong treatment with thyroid supplements.

Limber tail

Also known as 'limp tail' and 'Beagle tail', this is seen when a Beagle is unable to raise his tail, and shows discomfort when his tail is examined. It is thought to be the result of whiplash caused by violent shaking of the tail which bruises the nerve. In most cases, the problem rights itself within a couple of days but treatment with anti-inflammatories may be necessary.

Steroid responsive meningitis (SRM)

This is also referred to as 'Beagle pain syndrome' or 'stiff Beagle disease'. It is not unique to the Beagle, but it does seem to be over-represented in the breed when looking at the general dog population.

It is most commonly seen in Beagles between 8-18 months of ages and is characterised by a general lethargy, a stiff-legged gait and a reluctance to eat or drink. An affected dog may also have a high temperature. The condition is caused by inflammation of the blood vessels that supply the meninges (lining of the brain) and is thought to be the result of the immune system over-reacting. Treatment involves high doses of cortico-steroids.

Tumours

There are two types of tumour that most most commonly affect the Beagle – Lipomas and mast cell tumours. Lipomas are fatty lumps, which often develop in overweight dogs.

They are rarely malignant and removal is determined by how much they affect the dog.

Mast cell tumours can develop on relatively young dogs and the severity depends on individual cases. If you spot a lump developing on your Beagle, it is advisable to book an appointment with your vet so he can give your dog a full examination.

Summing up

It may give the pet owner cause for concern to find out about health problems that may affect their dog.

But it is important to bear in mind that acquiring some basic knowledge is an asset, as it will allow you to spot signs of trouble at an early stage.

Early diagnosis is very often the means to the most

effective treatment. Fortunately, the Beagle is a generally healthy and disease-free dog, with his only visits to the vet being annual check-ups.

In most cases, owners can look forward to enjoying many happy years with this affectionate and highly entertaining companion.

Useful addresses

Breed & Kennel Clubs
Please contact your Kennel Club to obtain contact information about breed clubs in your area.

UK
The Kennel Club (UK)
1 Clarges Street London, W1J 8AB
Telephone: 0870 606 6750
Fax: 0207 518 1058
Web: www.thekennelclub.org.uk

USA
American Kennel Club (AKC)
5580 Centerview Drive, Raleigh, NC 27606.
Telephone: 919 233 9767
Fax: 919 233 3627
Email: info@akc.org
Web: www.akc.org

United Kennel Club (UKC)
100 E Kilgore Rd, Kalamazoo,
MI 49002-5584, USA.
Tel: 269 343 9020
Fax: 269 343 7037
Web:www.ukcdogs.com/

Australia
Australian National Kennel Council (ANKC)
The Australian National Kennel Council is the administrative body for pure breed canine affairs in Australia. It does not, however, deal directly with dog exhibitors, breeders or judges. For information pertaining to breeders, clubs or shows, please contact the relevant State or Territory Body.

International
Fédération Cynologique Internationalé (FCI)
Place Albert 1er, 13, B-6530 Thuin, Belgium.
Tel: +32 71 59.12.38
Fax: +32 71 59.22.29
Web: www.fci.be/

Training and behavior
UK
Association of Pet Dog Trainers
Telephone: 01285 810811
Web: http://www.apdt.co.uk

Canine Behaviour
Association of Pet Behaviour Counsellors
Telephone: 01386 751151
Web: www.apbc.org.uk/

USA
Association of Pet Dog Trainers
Tel: 1 800 738 3647
Web: www.apdt.com/

American College of Veterinary Behaviorists
Web: http://dacvb.org/

American Veterinary Society of Animal Behavior
Web: www.avsabonline.org/

Australia
APDT Australia Inc
Web: www.apdt.com.au

For details of regional behaviorists, contact the relevant State or Territory Controlling Body.

Activities

UK

Agility Club
www.agilityclub.co.uk

British Flyball Association
Telephone: 01628 829623
Web: www.flyball.org.uk

USA

North American Dog Agility Council
Web: www.nadac.com

North American Flyball Association, Inc.
Tel/Fax: 800 318 6312
Web: www.flyball.org

Australia

Agility Dog Association of Australia
Tel: 0423 138 914
Web: www.adaa.com.au

NADAC Australia
Web: www.nadacaustralia.com
Australian Flyball Association
Tel: 0407 337 939
Web: www.flyball.org.au

International

World Canine Freestyle Organisation
Tel: (718) 332-8336
Web: www.worldcaninefreestyle.org

Health

UK

British Small Animal Veterinary Association
Tel: 01452 726700
Web: www.bsava.com

Royal College of Veterinary Surgeons
Tel: 0207 222 2001
Web: www.rcvs.org.uk

Alternative Veterinary Medicine Centre
Tel: 01367 710324
Web: www.alternativevet.org

USA

American Veterinary Medical Association
Tel: 800 248 2862
Web: www.avma.org

American College of Veterinary Surgeons
Tel: 301 916 0200
Toll Free: 877 217 2287
Web: www.acvs.org

Canine Eye Registration Foundation
The Veterinary Medical DataBases
1717 Philo Rd, PO Box 3007,
Urbana, IL 61803-3007
Tel: 217-693-4800
Fax: 217-693-4801
Web: www.vmdb.org

Orthopaedic Foundation of Animals
2300 E Nifong Boulevard
Columbia, Missouri, 65201-3806
Tel: 573 442-0418
Fax: 573 875-5073
Web: http://www.offa.org

American Holistic Veterinary Medical
Association
Tel: 410 569 0795
Web: www.ahvma.org

Australia

Australian Small Animal Veterinary
Association
Tel: 02 9431 5090
Web: www.asava.com.au

Australian Veterinary Association
Tel: 02 9431 5000
Web: www.ava.com.au

Australian College Veterinary Scientists
Tel: 07 3423 2016
Web: www.acvsc.org.au

Australian Holistic Vets
Web: www.ahv.com.au